CREATING THE DECLARATION OF INDEPENDENCE

CREATING THE DECLARATION OF INDEPENDENCE

David J. Shestokas

CONSTITUTIONALLY SPEAKING
Lemont, IL
www.shestokas.com

Questions? Comments?
DAVID@SHESTOKAS.COM
Twitter: @shestokas
© 2017 David J. Shestokas, J.D.
All Rights Reserved
ISBN: 978-0-9969281-2-0

Dedicated To All Who Seek To Understand
What Made America Great In The First Place

Constitutionally Speaking, Lemont, IL

Foreword

There have been few competitors to Thomas Jefferson in his ability to take the English language and express elegantly and simply an idea that is so profound that others write whole books to explain the same concept. A rival to Jefferson in that skill was a student of the Declaration of Independence: Abraham Lincoln.

To borrow Lincoln's method for calculating time, four score and three years after the Declaration of Independence in 1859, Lincoln said this about Jefferson:

"All honor to Jefferson--to the man who, in the concrete pressure of a struggle for national independence by a single people, had the coolness, forecast, and capacity to introduce into a merely revolutionary document, an abstract truth, applicable to all men and all times, and so to embalm it there, that to-day, and in all coming days, it shall be a rebuke and a stumbling-block to the very harbingers of re-appearing tyranny and oppression."

In the following pages you will discover a bit of how Jefferson came to embalm the abstract truth that stands in the way of despotism and tyranny and is the creed of the American mind in only 55 words. You will also learn a trick he used to get it done quickly.

I find fascinating the very human elements that are part of historic moments. Around our nation's capital there are huge monuments to Jefferson and Lincoln. In the presence of those works of art cut from marble and granite it is easy to forget that at one time they were flesh and blood human beings who worried about their family or had priorities that did not line up with the historic moment they were in.

Creating the Declaration of Independence takes you inside the mind of the man who formally proposed American independence, Richard Henry Lee and that of the man assigned to justify independence to the nations of the world, the soldiers of the Continental Army, and the American people, Thomas Jefferson. The decisions they made and the actions they took changed the world. This book provides insight into how they did it and provides an understanding into how lawyers like Jefferson work

The two main players in this story of *Creating the Declaration of Independence*, Lee and Jefferson, were taking risks that included the very real prospect of being beheaded.

Joining historical figures in such a moment, when we know their future and they do not, gives us a momentary sense of omniscience. Though we do not know our own future, we do know theirs.

I for one find that enjoyable. I hope you will as well.

You may also find value in my book, **Constitutional Sound Bites**, which explains America's Founding documents in a format familiar to 21st century readers. The Federalist Papers, by John Jay, Alexander Hamilton and James Madison explain the Constitution, but 21st Century Americans seldom read long newspaper essays. *Constitutional Sound Bites* addresses this by translating 18th Century English into a 21st Century format.

With over 150 questions and answers, *Constitutional Sound Bites* explains the philosophy, organization and purpose of America's Founding Documents and brings home the message that our shared heritage is not liberal nor conservative, Republican nor Democrat but American.

David J. Shestokas June, 2017

David J. Shestokas

Contents

- Foreword 1
- Introduction 7
- An Unprecedented Change to the World 13
- June 7, 1776 21
- Remembering History on an Historic Day 25
- The Gathering of Congress 29
- Concerns in Proposing Independence 35
- An Act of Treason 41
- Making the Case for Independence 47
- An Unprecedented Proposal 51
- Thoughts on The Way To City Tavern 53
- Jefferson & Adams Lay the Groundwork 59
- 1st Things 1st, the Virginia Constitution 65
- Adams Flatters Jefferson into Drafting the Declaration of Independence 73
- Jefferson Begins the Work 81
- Defining the American Mind 91
- The End of a Long Few Days 97
- Setting Quill to Parchment 101
- Jefferson the Lawyer at Work 107
- Eight Other Important Words 113
- The "Law of Nature and Nature's God" 117
- Recognition of Unenumerated Natural Rights in the U.S. Constitution 127

AFTERWORD 131
APPENDIX 133
The Declaration of Independence 133
Selected Bibliography 141
About David J. Shestokas 145

Introduction

When Americans celebrate publication of the Declaration of Independence on the Fourth of July, the country's national birthday, the celebration is dominated by parades, barbeques and fireworks. There is seldom reflection upon the many dramas preceding that fateful day, and little thought given to the meaning of the document. The party has taken over the substance at a time when the nation is divided in many ways. Spreading knowledge of our common heritage has the potential to bridge that divide and bring us together.

Usually overlooked during the July 4th celebrations is the seminal document that defines the American Creed central to our common heritage. How that document came to be, its meaning and worldwide impact on humanity are rare afterthoughts.

Part of the story of the genesis of the Declaration of Independence may best be told through two key players, both from Virginia, Richard Henry Lee and Thomas Jefferson. The story of Richard Henry Lee's Resolution for Independence and the selection of Thomas Jefferson to write a declaration in support of that resolution should be part of the knowledge of all Americans.

In the Declaration of Independence, Jefferson would condense 100 years of human wisdom that developed during a period alternately called the Enlightenment or the Age of Reason into a single extraordinary sentence that began: *"We hold these truths to be self-evident..."* With that sentence, Jefferson would give America her creed.

This creed, is built around ideas that if you consider them for even a moment are clearly true, or self-evident. Something is self-evident if it can be taken for granted and is in no need of proof or explanation. The Declaration of Independence is built around concepts that are undoubtedly true at first impression to any reasonable person.

Here are 55 crucial words from the Declaration of Independence: *"We hold these Truths to be self-evident, that all men are created equal, that they are endowed by their Creator with certain unalienable Rights that among these are Life, Liberty and the Pursuit of Happiness. That to secure these rights, Governments are instituted among Men, deriving their just powers from the consent of the governed..."*

The truths found in those 55 words may be accepted as self-evident in much of the world today. In 1776, when monarchies were the norm and slavery was legal, the accepted truth was that some were born to rule over others. The Declaration of Independence began to change acceptance of the idea that there were some entitled to be the masters of others, an idea that had permeated the human experience for 10,000 years. The change remains incomplete, but there has been monumental progress when one balances the 240 years since the Declaration against all of prior human history.

The opportunity for Jefferson to give us that creed would not have come, but for his fellow Virginian, Richard Henry Lee, who proposed to the Second Continental Congress that Britain's North American colonies declare their independence from the British crown.

The stories of Lee and Jefferson are intertwined and the result would change the world and create a country like none other before it.

Before the Declaration of Independence, nations would materialize in the haze of antiquity with their origins in a tribal past. The Declaration of Independence announced the establishment of a country that would be organized around shared ideas, not the exercise of raw force and power. Ideas that after the Declaration was issued, men and women would fight and die for, and continue to do so over two centuries later.

The Importance of the Declaration of Independence to the Constitution.

Study of the Declaration of Independence is crucial to understanding the Constitution. The Declaration provides definition and inspiration to the American journey. The Constitution provides mechanics and execution of the Declaration's ideals.

The Declaration told England's King George and the world why the colonies were separating from England. Importantly it also explained to the American people the philosophy of the new nation. Without an explanation to the people the new government would be without support, and one of the key tenets of the new American republic was that governments derive their power from the consent of the governed.

For the first time in world history a country would be guided by a philosophy not based upon force, but upon a shared view of government's purpose. The Declaration defined government's purpose to secure our inalienable rights. The Constitution's purpose is to secure the blessings of liberty. To understand the Declaration of Independence is to understand the Constitution.

The "self-evident" truths in the Declaration of Independence grow out of *"the Law of Nature and of Nature's God..."* The Natural Law referred to is recognized by the Constitution.

This recognition was critical to balance the need for an organized society and every individual's natural desire for freedom.

The United States was founded on a philosophy. That philosophy contained the truths that human beings are equal in their possession of natural rights, such as the rights to life, liberty and property. The Constitution is a set of rules to give life to the Declaration's central philosophy.

David J. Shestokas

An Unprecedented Change to the World

On June 7, 1776 Virginia's Richard Henry Lee stood up in the Second Continental Congress in Philadelphia and offered a resolution that would forever change the course of American and world history.

"Resolved: that these United Colonies are, and of right ought to be, free and independent States, that they are absolved from all allegiance to the British Crown, and that all political connection between them and the state of Great Britain is, and ought to be totally dissolved."

The congressional response to Lee's resolution was to create three committees. The first was to draft a Declaration of Independence. The second committee was to draft an agreement for a unified government among the colonies. The third was to create a standard treaty to be used for alliances and trade with foreign countries.

The North American colonies of the British Empire were about to embark upon a journey that had never been taken before. There was little guidance to be found in the history of nations.

David J. Shestokas

Previous Declarations: Replacing One King with Another

456 years earlier in 1320, the noblemen of Scotland (19 earls and 39 barons) had sent a letter to Pope John XXII, asking for relief from the rule of England's King Edward and recognition of Robert the Bruce as King of Scotland. The *Declaration of Arbroath* asked the pope to approve terminating Scottish allegiance to the British crown, and allow the Scots to swear allegiance to a different king. Richard Henry Lee and the Americans were not looking for a new king, they were looking to govern themselves.

In 1581, the people of the Netherlands terminated their allegiance to Spain's King Phillip. They did this by adopting the *Act of Abjuration*. The people declared that Phillip had abandoned his kingly duties to them and as a result they owed him no allegiance. The people of the Netherlands though, like the Scots 260 years earlier, were looking for a new king. They would get one, the Duke of Anjou, brother of the King of France. Again, this provided no guidance to the Americans.

In 1688, England itself declared the English throne had been vacated by King James II. James actually had been chased out of the country by the Dutch army led by the man who would become King William III. The 1688 English Declaration of Rights was employed to change kings in England, but set no precedent for independence from the British Empire. So, even this English experience was not an act of independence, but the act of trading one king for another. The American goal was entirely different and novel in world history.

The leaders of Revolutionary America were well versed in history and took heed to learn lessons from the past and strive to avoid mistakes that others had made. Richard Henry Lee's June 7th resolution to the Continental Congress, proposed the American colonies set a course to do something that had never been done before. They would absolve themselves of allegiance to King George, but not seek out a new king. They were determined to govern themselves.

The Committee of Five

Given the novelty of Lee's June 7th Resolution, and the dangers, Congress would need time to debate the resolution. At the time, members of Congress were delegates from the various colonies, and most had a duty to follow the instructions of the government of their home colony. On so important an issue as independence many would need time to consult and receive direction on how to vote on independence. Time was needed for debate and consultation, so a vote would not be taken until July 2nd.

Congress determined that in the event the resolution were adopted, it would be important to have a declaration in support of independence. On June 11, 1776, Benjamin Franklin, John Adams, Thomas Jefferson, Roger Sherman and Robert Livingston were appointed to the committee.

Adams and Jefferson met regarding a general outline of the declaration and Adams would ultimately convince Jefferson to do a draft. Jefferson created a draft. When Adams and Franklin reviewed Jefferson's work, Franklin suggested a single, but very important edit. Jefferson originally wrote *"We hold these truths to be sacred and undeniable..."* Franklin changed it to: *"We hold these truths to be self-evident..."*

On June 28, 1776, the committee sent its work to Congress. Over the next week Congress deleted about a fourth of the content and made a total of 85 edits. Jefferson referred to Congress' work as the *"the emasculation and mutilation of my Declaration of Independence."*

The congressional changes made to Jefferson's draft were primarily related to the list of grievances against King George. Some states had complaints that Jefferson had not listed that were added. He had also included a section blaming King George for the continued trade in slaves. That section was stricken in its entirety. Of note, there was not a single congressional change to the 55 words that Lincoln would later praise and have put the forces of tyranny and oppression on the defense throughout the world ever since.

Congress, on July 2, 1776, adopted Lee's original resolution for independence. It was the date that John Adams anticipated that: *"The Second Day of July 1776, will be the most memorable ... in the History of America ... It ought to be commemorated, as the Day of Deliverance by solemn Acts of Devotion to God Almighty. It ought to be solemnized with Pomp and Parade, with Shews, Games, Sports, Guns, Bells, Bonfires and Illuminations from one End of this Continent to the other from this Time forward forever more."*

The final editing of Jefferson's work was completed on July 4, 1776, and that was the date on the copies printed by Philadelphia printer John Dunlap that evening. As a result, John Adams predictions for a July 2nd holiday would ultimately take place on July 4th which became recognized as the national birthday.

Over 100 Declarations Since 1776

"The American Declaration of 1776 was the first in world history to identify sovereignty with independence."
David Armitage

From the 1215 Magna Carta, the 1320 Declaration of Arbroath, the 1581 Act of Abjuration, to the 1688 Declaration of Rights, when subjects were dissatisfied with their "sovereign" or royal ruler, the solution had been to make a deal with the current ruler or find a new one. The standard for a government was an empire principally controlled by a royal family. The American Declaration of Independence changed this, not just for America, but for the world.

There had never been a Declaration like the one issued on July 4. 1776. However, once it was issued, it set in motion worldwide change. In 1790, the people of the province of Flanders declared they were independent of the Austrian Emperor Joseph II. The successful slave revolt in Haiti was accompanied by a Declaration of Independence from France on January 1, 1804. There are now over 194 countries in the world. More than 100 of them came into being with the issuance of a document whose heritage can be traced to the Declaration of Independence.

There was no precedent for the action of the Second Continental Congress. There was no precedent to begin a country based upon the *"Laws of Nature and of Nature's God"*. The launching of a revolution by Great Britain's North American colonies, announced by the Declaration of Independence, became a precedent for the world.

With that in mind let us return to the summer of 1776.

David J. Shestokas

June 7, 1776

Richard Henry Lee awoke in Philadelphia on June 7, 1776 with both excitement and trepidation. This was to be a momentous day. Preparing for his day, he slipped the black satin glove on his left hand that he always wore in public. He daily cursed the rifle that had exploded eight years earlier that took four of his fingers. The cauterized stubs on his hand were a constant reminder of the year that he lost not only those fingers, but his beloved first wife, Anne. He reflected often on that "excellent lady" of the "most amiable goodness" gone in the "bloom of life". He did so momentarily before the importance of the day returned him to the present. There was work to be done.

Lee was a Virginia delegate to the Second Continental Congress of the United Colonies that had been meeting in Philadelphia since May, 1775. Despite the fact that armed conflict was ongoing between British soldiers and the Continental Army, and the immense popularity of the Thomas Paine pamphlet, *Common Sense,* which called for independence in no uncertain terms, Congress had carefully maintained a public posture that affirmed the colonies' allegiance to King George III.

In fact, the Congress and even George Washington, in command of the army, referred to the British troops they were fighting as "ministerial". By referring to the English soldiers as "ministerial" American leadership could maintain the political fiction that the armed conflict was with the English Prime Minister Lord Frederick North, his ministers and the English Parliament. This allowed the colonists to deny they were at war with the king. If the colonies were not battling King George, there might be a political solution to the conflict.

Many of Lee's fellow delegates hoped to reconcile with England. There was also the issue of treason and English law defined treason as betrayal of the king. Maintaining a position of royal allegiance, even while at war seemed a technical protection against a treason charge, and Congress was dominated by lawyers. A discussion of "independence" in so public a forum might be deemed treason, so "independence" had been a word tactfully avoided during congressional debate.

This day Lee would not only speak the word "independence" but submit a resolution to abandon the pretense of royal loyalty and run the risk of treason. The time had come to end the ruse, and fate had selected Richard Henry Lee to end it. He left for his work day in Congress.

As he walked to the Pennsylvania State House, where Congress met on the first floor, he thought of his conversations with Pennsylvania delegate John Dickinson. Dickinson opposed independence, and extolled the value of the colonies' British heritage and traditions. Among other things Dickinson brought up Magna Carta and the 1689 English Bill of Rights. Lee smirked at the thought of bringing up those subjects to support opposition to independence.

Lee's formal education in history at Wakefield Academy in Yorkshire, England, and his personal studies of the subject since had given him a healthy skepticism regarding the value of those two "symbols" of the British commitment to liberty.

David J. Shestokas

Remembering History on an Historic Day
Richard Henry Lee Considers
The Magna Carta

Like all good history students, Lee knew that in 1215 England's King John had set his royal seal to a document called "Magna Carta". The magnificent phrase in Latin is much less impressive in English: "Big Paper". The document had in fact been written on a very large piece of paper. King John sealed that document surrounded by the unsheathed knives of his own barons. The king had been trying to recoup his losses from an expensive and unsuccessful war with France's King Philip II by taxing English nobility.

The baronial families were having none of it, and responded to John's efforts by occupying London with their own knights. The barons sought neither independence nor freedom for England's population. They wanted a peace treaty with John that confirmed their place at the top of the English feudal system. The result was "Magna Carta" which turned out to be not very effective in keeping the peace.

Only a single Magna Carta clause of more than sixty in the document would have severely restricted the king's authority and King John was ultimately not ready for even that limit. A short three months after he set the royal seal to "Magna Carta", John pressed Pope Innocent II to annul the "shameful and demeaning agreement" that had been "forced upon the king by violence and fear." The Pope issued the annulment and civil war followed. The war only ended when King John died of dysentery in 1216.

Lee's reflection on the Magna Carta reminded him that whatever value Magna Carta may have for an Englishman in England, it had no value to an American in America.

What Value Was the "English Bill of Rights" to Americans?

As he turned the corner a block from the State House, Lee considered Dickinson's other example of the alleged British commitment to liberty: the "Glorious Revolution" and its 1689 "Bill of Rights". Again, Lee found the symbol lacking. In 1688 The Dutch Sovereign Willem sent his navy to England's shores and led his army into England and took control of London. England's King James II fled the country for France. Willem changed his name to William (to

Creating the Declaration of Independence

appear English, not Dutch) and with his Dutch troops occupying London became King of England.

Lee smiled at the irony that the English "Declaration of Rights", so revered by Englishmen, was an agreement with a Dutchman. To add to the insult to England, the Dutchman's wife, Queen Mary, was James II's daughter. So, this great symbol of English liberties was formed during a Dutch occupation of England, creating an "English" king who had chased out of England the father of his wife, largely because James was Roman Catholic. Ah yes, the great statement of English liberty.

Lee reminded himself to thank Mr. Dickinson for giving him another reason that Americans needed to be independent of a country so internally wracked with wars and royal intrigue. Dickinson's use of this "Glorious Revolution" to extoll the English tradition of liberty and a reason to postpone independence was as misleading as his invocation of Magna Carta.

Besides, the alleged "rights' from 1689 were not recognized by the British as belonging to Americans. The British abuses of the Americans for the last thirteen years were clear evidence of that. No, the time was now to be done with any pretense at reconciliation.

David J. Shestokas

The Gathering of Congress

Lee Arrives at the Pennsylvania State House

Having given due consideration to Dickinson's thoughts, Lee arrived at the Pennsylvania State House and entered the first floor meeting room promptly at 10 AM. It was the appointed hour for Congress to convene, but as was typically the case only a few delegates were present, and they were visiting with each other, few anxious to begin the day's proceedings. To Lee, it felt as though he was the single delegate interested to proceed with business.

Members arrived and Lee exchanged pleasantries. As Lee was about to take his seat he was approached by Massachusetts' John Adams. Adams had been the Congress' most vocal proponent of independence, and offered Lee his encouragement in proceeding with the resolution. While Lee had long been aware of Adams' support, the discussion with Adams today was most welcomed and cemented Lee's resolve to go forward.

Following the conversation with Adams, Lee sat down at Virginia's table. Soon he was joined by fellow Virginian

Thomas Jefferson. In the past Lee had talked with Jefferson about the lack of precedents in English history for independence, but the two were not talking much today. Jefferson had said good morning, but as was typical, little else. Though Jefferson was good with a quill, he was generally quiet otherwise. This day Lee was relieved to be sitting next to a man of so few spoken words like Jefferson, since Lee himself was lost in his own thoughts.

President John Hancock of Massachusetts arrived and settled into his chair at the front of the room. Hancock noted that enough members had arrived to call the meeting to order and did so. The Congress was now in session. This Friday assembly began by addressing ongoing business. Among the day's issues would be compensation for Mr. Charles Walker, owner of the sloop *Endeavour,* which had been commandeered by the colonies. Also under consideration was the status of military battalions raised in the colony of South Carolina.

This regular business gave Lee time to contemplate the momentous nature of his coming action and to consider how it had fallen to him to officially broach the subject of independence in the Congress.

Lee looked around at this gathering of leaders from the British North American colonies. He noted the absence of any

Creating the Declaration of Independence

Canadians, despite three attempts to involve them in the Congress. Lee himself had served on the committee for the first effort to communicate with the Canadians. Despite continuing congressional efforts and an American military excursion to Montreal, no response ever came from Quebec. The Canadian circumstance was of some regret to Lee, but surely no reason to delay independence.

Today Richard Henry Lee was firm in his resolve to bring the question of independence out into the open and beyond the conversations over an ale at the City Tavern.

An Awareness of History

Richard Henry Lee was aware of the historic importance of his contemplated action as the day's business of the Continental Congress proceeded. His own thoughts of history consumed him as he considered the implications of his impending act. Having considered the implications for future generations, he was suddenly keenly aware of the very real issues that would face him and his country very soon should his resolution ultimately win approval. That awareness returned him to the present and the ongoing proceedings around him.

And The Business at Hand and Its Meaning

Congressional discussion had moved on to a complaint regarding the gun powder coming out of Oswald Eve's mill. Since his 1761 election to the Virginia House of Burgesses Lee had been involved in the workings of a legislature. Lee knew that much of the time many matters felt mundane and often legislators failed to comprehend the true meaning of the things under consideration. Experience taught Lee that moments of high drama, though rare, were needed to call attention to the real import of seemingly otherwise dull legislative work.

What was the real meaning of colonial compensation to Mr. Walker for the *Endeavour?* Why were they discussing the status of army battalions raised in South Carolina? Why was the quality of Oswald Eve's gun powder important? As the delegates discussed the topics dispassionately, Lee wanted to shout out those questions followed by the answer. **The colonies were at war with Great Britain!!!** The time for high drama had long since passed, but Lee's resolve that it would begin soon was strengthened.

The discussions of the powder problem droned on. As Delegates Henry Wisner, Robert Treat Paine, and Robert Livingston were selected to look into the defects of Eve's powder,

Lee's patience began to wane, but he maintained legislative decorum and reflected how history had chosen him from among the colonial leaders to publicly and officially propose independence.

David J. Shestokas

Concerns in Proposing Independence

How Richard Henry Lee Came to Officially Propose Independence

Lee glanced at the fellow Virginian next to him, Thomas Jefferson. Nearly two years before, in 1774, Jefferson had articulated the justifications for civil war in his essay: *A Summary View of the Rights of British North America,* presented to the First Continental Congress. Jefferson had a talent with the written word and his composition had given Congress arguments that would defend an independence resolution.

John Adams had thought it wise an independence proposal should come from a southern colony, specifically Virginia. To Lee, Jefferson was the logical Virginian, but Tom was better with a quill than with a speech. Proposing a resolution required a speech. Though brilliant and multi-talented, public speaking was not among Jefferson's stronger skills. Jefferson had been notably quiet during his time in Congress and, at 33, was twelve years younger than Lee. Jefferson's silence and youth argued against his putting forth the resolution.

Having reminded himself why Jefferson was inappropriate, Lee looked across the room at John Adams. Adams had the rhetorical skills and the spirit to propose and defend a resolution for independence. Adams' Massachusetts had borne the brunt of British acts against the colonies. The colony had been the direct target of many of the King's abuses and Massachusetts militia were the first to shed blood the year before at Lexington and Concord. As an initial consideration, John Adams or another Massachusetts delegate would have been a common sense choice to introduce a resolution on independence.

Of course, initial thoughts and common sense were not always the grounds for political choices. Adams was both loud and obnoxious and little liked by his fellow delegates. John Hancock as president of the assembly, though from Massachusetts, could not propose such a resolution. Such an act would be inconsistent with his position. Besides, as Boston had been the hotbed of rebellion, a proposal from Massachusetts might be looked upon as trying to drag the other colonies into their fight.

No, neither Adams nor Hancock could effectively place the resolution before Congress.

As members discussed how Wisner, Paine and Livingston should investigate the substandard powder from the Eve mill, Lee's attention was drawn to the elderly man apparently asleep in the corner with his right foot wrapped in bandages and elevated on a chair in front of him. Pennsylvania's Dr. Benjamin Franklin (who had received honorary doctorates from the University of St. Andrews and Oxford University) was the most senior delegate supporting independence and generally respected among the members of Congress.

Franklin had often made Lee smile and had a talent for arriving at and expressing in the most self-effacing way extraordinarily complex matters. He would no doubt be able to define the urgency of independence for the delegates in a way difficult to dispute. Franklin had become the embodiment of this new people known as Americans. A resolution from him would receive respect and due consideration.

Lee recognized a major stumbling block for Franklin. Proposals were made to Congress on behalf of state delegations, not by delegates personally. Franklin's Pennsylvania delegation was split. John Dickinson's opposition to independence, hope for reconciliation and expressed belief in the benefits of English traditions placed him firmly at odds with Franklin. Although misleading, Dickinson's Magna Carta and Glorious Revolution invocations had swayed some to hesitate on independence.

While Lee doubted Dickinson's motives, Dickinson made it impossible for Franklin to offer a resolution on behalf of Pennsylvania. In thinking of the problematic Dickinson, Lee reminded himself that Dickinson and the old English symbols were respected among some delegates. This was something to remember in fashioning his own remarks. A reference to such symbols to support independence could aid the cause. He would wish to motivate, not alienate others.

Beyond the internal divisions, Pennsylvania was not the southern sponsor that Adams reasonably felt was needed for a resolution to be successful. Many in the south distrusted the

Yankees nearly as much as the British. Lee pondered for a moment if there were a southern candidate for this job besides Virginia.

North Carolina met the criteria of having southern trust and its April 12, 1776 Halifax Resolves made it a worthy colony to propose independence. The Resolves had been the first colonial instructions to a congressional delegation to vote in favor of independence. However, though The Fourth Provincial Congress of North Carolina had unanimously instructed Joseph Hewes, William Hooper, and John Penn to vote in favor of independence, they had not been authorized to initiate an independence resolution.

Having satisfied himself that there were no other alternatives, Lee thought with pride of his own Virginia, itself the victim of a brutal British attack that had destroyed the city of Norfolk six months earlier. This fight did clearly not belong to Massachusetts alone.

Virginia Instructs its Delegates
On Independence

Virginia had taken as strong a stand as any colony. On May 15th, the Virginia legislature had instructed its delegation unconditionally to propose and support American independence with the following language:

"Resolved, unanimously, That the Delegates appointed to represent this Colony in General Congress be instructed to propose to that respectable body to declare the United Colonies free and independent States, absolved from all allegiance to, or dependence upon, the Crown or Parliament of Great Britain..."

The Virginia instructions and the political and legal limits on others put Lee in this historic and precarious position. Though Lee was not a lawyer, he had studied law extensively. He was in a room dominated by lawyers. He and they were familiar with the English law of treason.

Lee understood an historic moment was approaching and that the moment had immense personal implications and dangers for him as well as for the millions in the colonies of British North America.

An Act of Treason

Richard Henry Lee Considers The Consequence of Treason

Lee was about to propose dissolving allegiance to the British King and forming alliances with enemies of the Crown. Though confident that all of Virginia was behind him, at that instant he would be standing alone in Congress proposing treason. The British penalty for treason was exceptionally heinous. Sir William Blackstone described it as follows:

"THE punishment of high treason in general is very solemn and terrible. 1. That the offender be drawn to the gallows, and not be carried or walk; though usually a sledge or hurdle is allowed, to preserve the offender from the extreme torment of being dragged on the ground or pavement. 2. That he be hanged by the neck, and then cut down alive. 3. That his entrails be taken out, and burned, while he is yet alive. 4. That his head be cut off. 5. That his body be divided into four parts. 6. That his head and quarters be at the king's disposal."

 The punishment for treason in the law was indeed "very solemn" and terrible". So solemn and terrible that it was difficult at times to believe such punishment would actually be inflicted. Richard Henry Lee was aware like the other members of Congress that beheading was a very real possibility.

Lee was familiar with the story of Dr. Joseph Warren. Warren had been the personal doctor of John Adams and his family and a member of the Sons of Liberty the group led by John's cousin, Sam Adams. On April 18, 1775 Warren had been the one to send Paul Revere to spread the alarm to the countryside. He had also served as President of the Massachusetts Provincial Congress and a Major General in the Massachusetts Militia.

Lee knew that neither political office nor high military rank spared General Warren the ultimate indignity. Warren received a British musket ball to his face at Bunker Hill nearly a year ago on June 17, 1775. A British execution squad mutilated Warren with their bayonets and cut off his head for display on a spit. The threat of beheading for treason was not just in the king's law books, it was very real.

Richard Henry Lee was about to commit treason against the British crown. The possibility of being hanged, gutted, burned alive and beheaded did much to focus his thoughts. It did not dissuade him from his course of action.

The day had been one of deep contemplation for Richard Henry Lee. He had begun the day by cursing the rifle that misfired and took four fingers from his hand. He had spent time in fond reverie with thoughts of his departed wife Anne. Turning to the business of the day he had considered the resolution for independence and how fate had chosen him to offer it. The possible consequence of that resolution had brought visions of being gutted, burned and beheaded for treason and an uncomfortable intrusion on his consciousness. The time to put himself at risk of the horrifying punishment was near.

Time to Propose the Resolution For Independence

The congressional discussions regarding the powder problems at Eve's mill came to a close. Richard Henry Lee sought recognition from President Hancock. As he did so, Lee one last time reflected upon being hung, mutilated, burned, and beheaded then put those thoughts aside in the knowledge that no other delegate was in a position to move the Continental Congress toward independence. He rose and placed before Congress the following resolution:

"Resolved, That these United Colonies are, and of right ought to be, free and independent States, that they are absolved from all allegiance to the British Crown, and that all political connection between them and the State of Great Britain is, and ought to be, totally dissolved.

That it is expedient forthwith to take the most effectual measures for forming foreign Alliances.

That a plan of confederation be prepared and transmitted to the respective Colonies for their consideration and approbation."

Quick Support from John Adams, Hesitation from the Rest of Congress

John Adams would quickly second the resolution and join Lee in the treasonous act.

Other delegates did not offer immediate support. Their actual response was a motion to delay consideration of Lee's proposal to declare independence. Though Lee understood that many delegations had not received instructions on independence, he thought the time to declare was now. The discussions of naval vessels, South Carolina troops and concerns over gun powder had clearly demonstrated the need. An army and a navy needed something to fight for.

Though frustrated by the proposed delay, he knew if there were to be a delay, those delegates seeking independence instructions from their states needed a strong reminder regarding the arguments in favor of independence. Debates on the resolution and proposed postponement took place on June 8th and 10th. During that time, Lee took the opportunity to make the case for independence.

David J. Shestokas

Making the Case for Independence

Richard Henry Lee's Argument for Independence

Lee forcefully warned that independence was inevitable, that the historic moment was upon them, the people were ready and that postponement would be folly:

"The time will certainly come when the fated separation between the mother country and these colonies must take place whether you will or no, for it is so decreed by the very nature of things by the progressive increase of our population, the fertility of our soil, the extent of our territory, the industry of our countrymen, and the immensity of the ocean which separates the two countries.

And if this be true, as it is most true, who does not see that the sooner it takes place, the better? -- that it would be the height of folly not to seize the present occasion when British injustice has filled all hearts with indignation, inspired all minds with courage, united all opinions in one, and put arms in every hand? And how long must we traverse three thousand miles of a stormy sea to solicit of arrogant and insolent men either counsel or commands to regulate our domestic affairs? From what we have already achieved it is easy to presume what we shall hereafter accomplish.

Experience is the source of sage counsels and liberty is the mother of great men. Have you not seen the enemy driven from Lexington by citizens armed and assembled in one day? Already their most celebrated generals have yielded in Boston to the skill of ours. Already their seamen repulsed from our coasts wander over the ocean, the sport of tempests and the prey of famine. Let us hail the favorable omen and fight not for the sake of knowing on what terms we are to be the slaves of England but to secure to ourselves a free existence to found a just and independent government.

Why do we longer delay? Why still deliberate? Let this most happy day give birth to the American Republic. Let her arise not to devastate and conquer but to re-establish the reign of peace and the laws. The eyes of Europe are fixed upon us; she demands of us a living example of freedom that may contrast by the felicity of her citizens with the ever-increasing tyranny which desolates her polluted shores.

She invites us to prepare an asylum where the unhappy may find solace and the persecuted repose. She entreats us to cultivate a propitious soil where that generous plant which first sprang up and grew in England but is now withered by *the poisonous blasts of Scottish tyranny may revive and flourish, sheltering under its salubrious and interminable shade all the unfortunate of the human race.*

This is the end presaged by so many omens; by our first victories; by the present ardor and union; by the flight of Howe and the pestilence which broke out among Dunmore's people; by the very winds which baffled the enemy's fleets and transports, and that terrible tempest which engulfed seven hundred vessels upon the coast of Newfoundland. If we are not this day wanting in our duty to our country, the names of the American legislators will be placed, by posterity, at the side of those of Theseus, of Lycurgus, of Romulus of Numa, of the three Williams of Nassau, and of all those whose memory has been and will be forever dear to virtuous men and good citizens."

Postponing the Vote on Independence

There would not be a quick vote. It would be postponed for three weeks for two purposes. First, to provide time for delegates to consult with their home states on independence instructions and second for a committee to draft a declaration to be issued in the event the independence resolution were adopted.

Richard Henry Lee was not on the drafting committee. Lee had to return to Virginia due to the illness of his second wife, who like his first, was named Anne. As Virginia proposed the resolution for independence, it was appropriate that a Virginian be on the committee to draft the declaration that might be issued in support of the resolution. On June 11th, four days after Lee offered his resolution, Benjamin Franklin nominated Thomas Jefferson to be that Virginian.

Congress voted to delay consideration of Lee's resolution until July 1, 1776.

Though there were debates, discussions and proposals, others in Congress would not officially join Adams and Lee on the slippery steps to torture and beheading for at least three weeks.

An Unprecedented Proposal

The action proposed by Lee was unprecedented in world history. In 1776, the world was made up of empires. The title assigned to a head of government varied around the world. An empire might have a king, a czar, an emperor, a pharaoh or a sultan. These rulers would have power sharing arrangements with an aristocracy or nobility. Territory and peoples would be traded among these empires by agreement or war. For most people in the world, the change of a ruler meant simply trading one individual or small group of individuals with absolute power for a different person or group with the same power.

Through human history there had been changes in the relationships between the principal ruler and others sharing power over the ruled. The changes reflected little change for the ruled. There have been documents to memorialize the changes, like the Magna Carta and the 1689 English Bill of Rights, that have become quite celebrated, attaining nearly sacred status. These documents and others have been touted as precursors or inspirations for the change proposed for the American colonies. Such analogies were tenuous at best.

The actions that the Americans would take following Richard Henry Lee's resolution would be like nothing that had happened before. The resolution for American independence proposed creating a nation *without a ruler*. That was not an evolution from English tradition, it was a rejection of English tradition.

Something exceptional was happening in America in 1776

Thoughts on The Way To City Tavern

Five days after Lee put forth his resolution, Thomas Jefferson left the June 12, 1776 meeting of the Second Continental Congress with mixed emotions. His walk from the Pennsylvania State House took him east on Chestnut Street toward the City Tavern. He knew the route well. He had had many informal meetings there with his fellow delegates and was well acquainted with both the fine food and atmosphere. Besides its other qualities, the proprietors made it convenient by allowing him an open account.

The walk was short, a couple blocks on Chestnut, right on Third to the half-block cut-off to Walnut. Though short, the walk took him the opposite direction from his apartment at Seventh and High Street. This meeting would mean a delay in his return to the apartment and on this evening that was a bit annoying. Very significant things were happening back home in Virginia.

The City Tavern get-together was important, but there were so many important things these days. It seemed every time he turned around he was being appointed to another committee at this Congress and Virginia was in the midst of setting up a new government to replace the old colonial order, most notably drafting its constitution for transition from a colony to a state.

David J. Shestokas

Longing to be In Virginia

How he wished to be in Virginia. Jefferson had only been in Philadelphia since May 14th and now he'd been appointed to a committee to draft a declaration in support of a resolution made the previous Friday by his fellow Virginian Richard Henry Lee. Lee had introduced the resolution for independence to the Continental Congress last week, and now had to return to Virginia due to the illness of his wife.

Jefferson considered that. His mother had died on March 31, and he had suffered with severe headaches for six weeks following her death. His own wife was not well enough to make the weeklong trip to Philadelphia.

For both personal and professional reasons he envied Lee and his return to Virginia. Jefferson's envy grew out of his knowledge that on May 15th, the day after he had arrived in Philadelphia, the Virginia Convention in Williamsburg had taken two momentous acts.

Virginia had declared its own independence from the British Crown and sent instructions to the delegates in Philadelphia to introduce a resolution for American independence. Lee had acted on those instructions. Now Virginia was in the midst of drafting and adopting its own constitution. Virginia was where the real action was.

Jefferson had done several drafts of a Virginia constitution himself. His old friend and mentor George Wythe was going back to Virginia in a day or so, and Jefferson was intent on sending his ideas for the Virginia constitution with him. Jefferson hoped his thoughts would find their way into the new Virginia government, but chances would be better if he were there to defend them. There were certainly things of importance in Philadelphia, but Virginia was foremost in Jefferson's thoughts.

On Working with Pennsylvania's John Dickinson

As he made his way to City Tavern, there were other delegates on the street, many with the same destination. It was typical after sessions for many to gather there to talk of the day's events. Often members of the multitude of committees would meet and pursue their committee work at the tavern. John Adams was known to say that City Tavern was where the real work was done.

Jefferson noted Pennsylvania's John Dickinson walking ahead of him with Roger Sherman of Connecticut and Robert Livingston of New York. The three seemed in deep conversation. They had been appointed to a committee to address the second part of Lee's resolution, drafting a plan of government for the united colonies in the event Congress agreed to independence.

Jefferson imagined Dickinson, Sherman and Livingston were already exchanging thoughts on constructing a national government. Sherman and Livingston had been appointed to both Jefferson's declaration committee and Dickinson's confederation committee. Sherman and Livingston had chosen to discuss confederation. Jefferson took this as an indication of the low level of importance that a written declaration of independence held in their minds.

Jefferson and Dickinson had "worked" together nearly a year earlier on another Continental Congress document. Jefferson's experience with Dickinson in creating the "*Declaration of the Causes and Necessity for Taking Up Arms*" had been a bit contentious.

Jefferson's fellow Virginian George Washington had been made commander-in-chief June 19, 1775. There was a need to explain to many, especially Washington's troops and potential recruits, why the colonists had formed an army. On June 23, 1775, Congress appointed a committee for drafting a document containing reasons the colonies needed their own army.

After South Carolina's John Rutledge had drafted an unacceptable document in a single day, Jefferson and Dickinson were added to the committee. Jefferson remembered the less than collegial "collaboration" with Dickinson in the two weeks it took to get a document in order.

Those two weeks were not really collaborative. Jefferson had created a document to replace Rutledge's work, and gave it to Dickinson for review. To Jefferson, Dickinson's review criticized not only the style but the substance. Dickinson had found Jefferson to be too provocative of the English. Too provocative? Jefferson scoffed at that thought.

In April, 1775 at Lexington and Concord 49 Americans had died at the hands of the British. On June 17, 1775 at Bunker Hill, the redcoats killed 115 Americans. Just over a week after Bunker Hill, Dickinson wanted Jefferson to soften his language in a document explaining why America needed an army.

From that time, in July, 1775 until this moment, Dickinson was the leader of those hesitant to be blunt about the colonists' complaints with British rule. In Jefferson's mind, Dickinson was among those who bore responsibility for the fact that the American colonies were not yet independent.

As Jefferson recalled that experience in "working" with Dickinson, he was glad Dickinson was not on this declaration committee.

David J. Shestokas

Jefferson & Adams Lay the Groundwork

Joining John Adams at City Tavern

Jefferson trailed Dickinson, Sherman and Livingston into City Tavern. He watched them join other members of the Confederation Committee to talk over ideas for a national government. Over in a corner he saw John Adams seated alone. Jefferson joined Adams.

Jefferson asked Adams: "Will Dr. Franklin be joining us?" Benjamin Franklin was the fifth member of the Declaration Committee, but had seldom been at sessions of late due to a severe flare up of the gout in his right leg.

Adams shook his head without looking up from the notes he was reading. "I'm afraid we will not be blessed by either Ben's humor or wisdom early on in this task. I understand his suffering is intolerable."

Jefferson nodded acknowledgement and gestured to the table with the Confederation Committee. "What about Sherman and Livingston?"

Still concentrating on his notes, Adams replied, "Livingston is on this committee in the hope of getting New York involved and committed. Why their assembly won't commit on independence is beyond comprehension. Washington and the army are in New York City building up the defenses and there's reason to believe the British Navy is sailing from Halifax to New York. Despite that I expect little from Livingston."

"And Sherman?" Jefferson inquired, knowing that although Adams' abrasive manner was disliked by many, he seemed to know everything that was happening.

"It's enough for the declaration to have the input of this New Englander. While I admire Roger's pragmatism, his skill at motivating men with the written word has its limits. We will pay Roger the appropriate courtesy, but for the moment, it's us." Adams himself was thinking he wished to be concentrating on another of his over two dozen committee assignments, particularly as he had been appointed that day to the Board of War and Ordnance. It appeared things were soon to literally explode in New York.

Jefferson considered Adams' response. Adams was slow with compliments. Jefferson took Adams's comment on the shortcomings of Sherman's writing to be an endorsement of his own. In a separate vein Jefferson found writing by committee frustrating. A small committee with the limited involvement of others for such an assignment pleased him. Words came better in a solitary environment, with intermittent mental refreshment from playing his violin.

Jefferson, in deference to the man eight years his senior and so intimately involved with the workings of Congress, asked: "How do you suggest we proceed?"

Adams replied, "First we should order some refreshment and food." They did, and began a discussion that would have impact around the world.

First Considerations

Having placed their order for ale and a serving of the meal being served at City Tavern that evening, Thomas Jefferson and John Adams returned to the reason they had met: moving forward on a document to announce American independence.

Adams, took the lead: "Let's consider the form this declaration should take. There's little sense in starting over from scratch. We're both lawyers, and I think we can find an effective model for explaining why the colonies are breaking from England. It's also likely to be useful to look at the available, though limited historical parallels. If we lay out a general structure first we can go from there. Whatever general approach we choose, it's important to remember this declaration must speak to many audiences."

Listening to Adams, Jefferson reflected upon how "declarations" were constructed through history, particularly those lodging complaints against a king. The Scots had done it in 1320, the Dutch had in 1581, and the English in 1689.

The Declaration of Independence Takes Shape

Though their food and drink had been served, Jefferson and Adams continued to talk as the ale got warm and the food cold. They concentrated on their task: building a declaration for independence. Given their legal training, it was natural for them to agree upon a format for the declaration similar to a civil complaint used to start a lawsuit:

    1. A preamble or "whereas" statement explaining the purpose of the document

    2. A statement of law/philosophy that states the basis for the proposed action

    3. A list of grievances against the king

    4. Prior actions taken in response to the king's acts.

    5. Apply the law/philosophy to the actions to arrive at the conclusion that independence is the appropriate remedy to the grievances.

It was an outline the two lawyers understood, and thought, so would the intended audiences: the leadership of the other colonies; the governments of France, Spain and England; the

Continental Army in New York and elsewhere preparing to defend against expected British attacks; and the American people.

Upon completing the outline and identifying the audience Jefferson remarked to Adams: "The form is familiar, the audience is challenging."

Adams replied: "It's just a much larger jury, and we put a great deal of trust in juries."

Jefferson added: "The largest jury is the American people. Ultimately it will need to be an expression of the American mind and make clear that our independence is simply common sense." Adams nodded his agreement.

Their selection of form complete, Adams indicated he would convey, out of courtesy, their discussion to the other committee members. Adams asked Jefferson to begin thinking about the content to fill in the form. With this stage of the process finished, they ate their meal, mostly in silence.

As Jefferson drained his stein he became aware of others waiting to speak with Adams. This was unsurprising, considering Adams' many committee memberships. Jefferson thought to himself: "He's not much liked, but he's surely respected."

Jefferson stood to take his leave. The five foot seven inch Adams showed no notice of the height of the six foot two inch

Jefferson and stood as well. They shook hands and Jefferson left City Tavern to return to the apartment he rented from bricklayer Jacob Graff.

1st Things 1st, the Virginia Constitution

Something Really Important: The Virginia Constitution

Walking to Graff House, named for the man who built it, Jefferson thought briefly of his mother's death a little more than two months earlier, and the debilitating headaches he endured for the six weeks following her apparent stroke at 56. He forced his thoughts to return to the present, as Virginia was writing a constitution and the colonies were on the verge of independence and he was in the middle of it. Clearly the declaration project with Adams had *some* importance, but the first order of business for him was Virginia.

Jefferson really wished he were in Virginia instead of Philadelphia and involved in this declaration business. He would put off considering the declaration for now, and try to find a way to contribute to something truly significant, the constitution of Virginia.

During that walk to his apartment from his meeting with John Adams at City Tavern, Thomas Jefferson's mind wandered. He thought of his mother and her recent passing, his hopes that recovery from his six-week ordeal of headaches was permanent and the Adams meeting, which had been a good start on the declaration project. In the end, as always, his mind returned to the Virginia Constitutional Convention in Williamsburg.

Jefferson was unaware that even while he was sitting in the Continental Congress on June 12, 1776 and later meeting with Adams, the Virginia Convention had adopted George Mason's Declaration of Rights. Jefferson wanted his own ideas on protecting the rights of Virginians and structuring their new government to be part of the debate taking place in Williamsburg. Arriving at the Graff house he resolved to do his best to get his thoughts to Williamsburg as quickly as possible.

Jefferson's Virginia Constitution

After climbing the stairs and entering his second floor apartment he picked up and read over the constitution he had drafted for Virginia. He thought about how his note to Thomas Nelson of May 16th and his suggestion that the Virginia delegation be recalled to participate in the state's convention had gone unanswered.

The Virginia constitution was, after all, as he had written Nelson: *"the whole object of the present controversy; for should a bad government be instituted for us in future it had been as well to have accepted at first the bad one offered to us from beyond the water without the risk and expence of contest."* His request had gone unanswered.

He wanted to be in Williamsburg to defend his ideas on government. Those wishes aside, the reality was that his long mentor and fellow Virginian, George Wythe was leaving in the morning and if Jefferson hoped to have his thoughts arrive in Williamsburg in a timely manner he needed to get a satisfactory draft to George.

After an initial review of his draft constitution, he relaxed with his violin briefly, but knew the urgency of putting quill to parchment. Jefferson sat down in his recently invented swivel chair, spun around a bit marveling at his own ingenuity and then returned for a detailed reading of his draft Virginia Constitution to assure himself that specific items were included and clear.

He wished to make certain there were provisions for unambiguous rights. He reviewed his proposed language:

Religion
All persons shall have full and free liberty of religious opinion; nor shall any be compelled to frequent or maintain any religious institution.

Arms
No freeman shall be debarred the use of arms [within his own lands].
Standing Armies
There shall be no standing army but in time of actual war.

Free Press
Printing presses shall be free, except so far as by commission of private injury cause may be given of private action.

Jefferson thought inclusion of these items was crucial. He truly wanted the new Virginia Constitution to include a provision that would mark the beginning of the end of slavery. This was a point he knew would require a personal argument, and regretted his current assignment would keep him from making it. He thought the wording good. It recognized the reality of slavery in Virginia, but prevented the introduction of any new slaves, and this would ultimately lead to extinction of the "institution":

Slaves
"No person hereafter coming into this county shall be held within the same in slavery under any pretext whatever."

Consistent with what he would soon write about the equality of all men, he thought Virginia should recognize rights in the lands of Native Americans, and his draft included that idea:

Indian Lands

"No lands shall be appropriated until purchased of the Indian native proprietors; nor shall any purchases be made of them but on behalf of the public, by authority of acts of the General assembly to be passed for every purchase specially."

To prevent Virginians from being the subjects of a permanent ruling class, his proposal regarding the Virginia Senate Jefferson provided for three year terms and included this clause:

Limits on Virginian Senators

"When once removed, they shall be forever incapable of being re-appointed to that house."

Jefferson remembered the various excuses the British had for avoiding juries and the American belief that juries decide every controversy. The right to a jury trial in all cases and with in-court witnesses was crucial:

Juries

"All facts in causes whether of Chancery, Common, Ecclesiastical, or Marine law, shall be tried by a jury upon evidence given viva voce, in open court..."

A Prescient Thought

Jefferson's review of his draft Virginia Constitution confirmed the most essential ideas were included and it was ready for Wythe to take to Virginia. During his final review he reread the preamble he had written. The explanation as to why Virginia needed a constitution included a list of King George's abuses. Before extinguishing the candles, he thought: "Hmm... there's something that can be used for the grievance section of the declaration Adams and I had discussed."

Lee Returns to Virginia, Jefferson is stuck in Philadelphia

The next morning Jefferson made certain George Wythe had Jefferson's draft of the Virginia constitution. Jefferson could trust Wythe to deliver his draft Virginia constitution to the Williamsburg Convention. Jefferson had served as Wythe's legal apprentice for five years following his studies at William and Mary College.

Wythe's traveling companion to Virginia was Richard Henry Lee, the man Jefferson most envied at the moment. Since Lee had introduced the resolution for independence to the Continental Congress a week earlier, he would have been the logical choice as the Virginian to serve on the declaration of independence committee. Jefferson thought that but for the illness of Lee's wife, he could be going to Williamsburg where he could have a greater impact on history than being stuck in Philadelphia and assigned to that committee, working on this declaration that most considered necessary but unimportant.

Jefferson wondered why fate had conspired to keep him away from Virginia. With the independence vote not scheduled until July 1st, he would likely be trapped here for some time.

By mid-morning of June 13, 1776 Thomas Jefferson had done all he could to impact the coming constitution of Virginia. He had reviewed his proposed constitution to be certain all needed provisions to protect the people's liberty were included. The first thing that morning he made certain that Wyeth would deliver his proposed constitution to the Virginia convention. Despite Jefferson's desire to be in Virginia, he was

David J. Shestokas

in Philadelphia and had to tend to his duties in the Second Continental Congress.

Adams Flatters Jefferson into Drafting the Declaration of Independence

Back to the Business of
The Continental Congress

The morning of June 14, 1776 Jefferson arrived at the Pennsylvania State House as President John Hancock called the morning session of the Second Continental Congress to order a little after 10 AM. Though Lee's resolution on independence was pending, there was other business to be addressed. On this day the Congress would add to John Adams' ever increasing work load. Adams was appointed chairman of the Board of War and Ordnance.

When Jefferson had met with Adams the day before about the independence declaration, they had agreed to follow up today. With the increasing pressures on Adams' time it was unclear that he and Jefferson would have the chance to talk. At the lunch break, Jefferson saw a group of delegates congregating in the area outside the assembly space.

Jefferson's height allowed him to look over the group and see the short Adams in the center. Jefferson could not tell if Adams was aware of Jefferson's presence or if Adams could see past the men around him. Jefferson was about to walk away when Adams looked up, sensed the towering presence and gestured for Jefferson to wait. Adams concluded his conversations and the two men greeted each other.

In short order, as Adams was quick to get to the point, they resumed their discussion of the independence declaration.

Who will Draft the Declaration?

Adams began: "In the midst of everything I tracked down Sherman, Livingston and Franklin. I've told them of our conversation regarding the structure of the declaration. They are agreed with the general articles that should be included and the approach we discussed."

Though Jefferson was keenly aware of Adams' ever increasing responsibilities, he again thought it proper to defer to the older man, "Then you will no doubt work from those points and begin a draft of the declaration."

John Adams did not consider drafting this declaration of independence a particularly important piece of work. On May 15th a proposal of his own had been adopted by the Congress. Adams had written the preamble to Congress' advice to the states about the need for forming new governments and adopting new constitutions:

"Whereas his Britannic Majesty, in conjunction with the lords and commons of Great Britain, has, by a late act of Parliament, excluded the inhabitants of these United Colonies from the protection of his crown; And whereas, no answer, whatever, to the humble petitions of the colonies for redress of grievances and reconciliation with Great Britain, has been or is likely to be given; but, the whole force of that kingdom, aided by foreign mercenaries, is to be exerted for the destruction of the good people of these colonies; And whereas, it appears absolutely irreconcileable to reason and good Conscience, for the people of these colonies now to take the oaths and affirmations necessary for the support of any government under the crown of Great Britain, and it is necessary that the exercise of every kind of authority under the said crown should be totally suppressed, and all the powers of government exerted, under the authority of the people of the colonies, for the preservation of internal peace, virtue, and good order, as well as for the defence of their lives, liberties, and properties, against the hostile invasions and cruel depredations of their enemies"

John Adams was certain that history would recognize him as the actual author of the document that declared independence, and so this new declaration was simply a small detail.

Adams, believing his own place in history secure and conscious of his work load, was anxious to delegate this minor assignment. He had anticipated Jefferson's suggestion and was prepared with a reply.

"Thomas, there are many reasons that the drafter should be you and not me. Here are the best five:

1. You are a Virginian, and I'm from Massachusetts.
2. You are a southern man and I am a northerner.
3. The obnoxious nature of my zeal in promoting independence would cause any draft of mine to undergo great scrutiny and criticism from Congress that a draft from you would not receive.
4. Though I have yet to hear you utter three sentences in a single instance during sessions in congress, I have a great opinion of the elegance of your pen and little of the elegance of my own pen.
5. Finally and most importantly, you can write ten times better than I can."

Jefferson paused at the lavish praise Adams had just conferred upon him. While flattered, several thoughts crossed his mind. Richard Henry Lee, sponsor of the independency resolution, had just left for Virginia. The sponsor's participation at this point would be customary, but Lee had left town to care for his ailing wife. Roger Sherman had also been selected for the Board of War and Ordnance. Sherman's priorities did not include writing an independence declaration. Roger Livingston's presence on the declaration committee had been an effort to compliment New York. Dr. Franklin was in pain every day, and as Franklin would later confide, he was not in the habit of writing things that would be edited by a committee.

Drafting the declaration was not a particularly sought after assignment and it was now falling upon Jefferson.

Smiling inwardly to himself since he understood the motive behind Adams' unrestrained compliments, Jefferson replied with a bit of understatement, "Well, if you are decided I will do as well as I can."

David J. Shestokas

Setting Priorities for the Declaration

Following Jefferson's acceptance, the men reviewed the declaration's format that they discussed the day before. This review included the necessary points for each audience for the document. The leadership and citizens of the wavering colonies were the most important audience in the short term. Without their votes and support there would be no independence.

The Continental Army and potential recruits were just as crucial. It would need to give voice to what had become known since Lexington and Concord simply as "The Cause". Jefferson and Adams had no illusions that King George and Parliament would read the declaration with approval. The declaration would need to inspire the sacrifice of blood and treasure to turn its words into reality. There was a need to motivate men to die.

The declaration would need to reflect the beliefs that Americans felt in their hearts. This document was not to "convince" Americans of the justness of independence, but rather give expression to the thinking in their minds that had already developed. The goal, as Adams put it, was to take agreed upon American republican principles and "cloath them in a proper Dress".

Upon completing a review of the audience for the declaration and the goals it needed to achieve, Adams concluded the discussion, "Very well, when you have drawn it up we will have a meeting."

David J. Shestokas

Jefferson Begins the Work

The Act of Inventing: Thought Process for a Chair or a Country

Though Congress would have an afternoon session, Jefferson returned to Graff house to consider the declaration. Once in his apartment with quill and parchment he wrote an outline. With that complete he turned in his chair and looked out the window. He took pleasure in considering his unique chair, his invention with window casters allowing the seat to "swivel" on the base. He smiled as he considered whether the thinking required to create a chair differed any from that needed to create a country.

His wish to be in Virginia returned for a moment, but it was time to turn to working on his assignment, a declaration to explain the reasons for American independence. He became reconciled that he would not be in Virginia to participate in the drafting of the Virginia Constitution, and that his lot would be to draft a declaration to explain the American move to independence if the resolution for independency were adopted on July 1st.

He was sitting in a distinctively American chair, about to embark upon the creation of a distinctively American declaration. Though the goal was to capture American ideas, he remembered yesterday's conversation with Adams and the mental note he'd made of historical precedents that may have a connection to this American declaration.

Jefferson wished he had access to his Monticello library. In leaving Monticello for his journey to Philadelphia, Jefferson had not anticipated the assignment of drafting a declaration defending independence. Though his library contained books by many great thinkers and historical writings he had brought "neither book nor pamphlet" related to such an undertaking. He did have available yesterday's *Philadelphia Gazette* that had published George Mason's proposed Virginia Declaration of Rights.

He relaxed a bit with his violin to clear his mind and then began making notes on the historical comparisons, since there might be some guidance on how to proceed from antiquity. It was time to look for that guidance in historical events.

Magna Carta

In recent days, Jefferson had discussed with Richard Henry Lee how Pennsylvania's John Dickinson so often invoked *Magna Carta*.

He was of a mind with Lee in thinking that document was the result of the English nobility seeking a secure place in the feudal system, negotiated at knife point. Jefferson considered the politics of *Magna Carta*'s resurrection over 400 years after it had been annulled by the pope.

In the early 17th Century, The Lord Chief Justice Edward Coke had convinced King James I that *Magna Carta* was still in effect as a limit on the King's power. Jefferson thought it likely James couldn't read *Magna Carta,* since it was written in Latin. Coke could read Latin and the King relied upon him to explain what the document meant.

Magna Carta had never been the source of any rights, but Jefferson admired Lord Coke's ingenuity in selling the importance of *Magna Carta* to King James.

He agreed with Lee that a document signed by King John under threat to his life, revoked by the pope, forgotten for 400 years and used by Lord Coke to enhance his own authority at the expense of King James was not a likely place to look for inspiration in constructing a declaration of American independence.

The Declaration of Arbroath

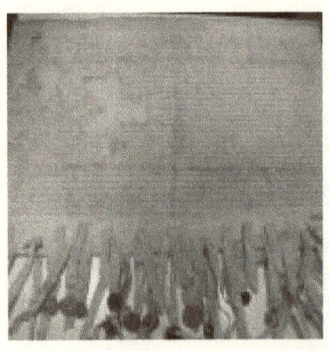

Jefferson moved from that ancient document to his studies with Professor William Small at William and Mary College in Williamsburg. Professor Small was a Scotsman from Aberdeen who had introduced Jefferson to many subjects and philosophers, among them John Locke. Small was a professor of philosophy with a pride in his Scottish heritage.

Small had brought to Jefferson's attention a document of particular pride to Scotsmen, the 1320 Declaration of Arbroath. Over 450 years before Jefferson was given this task, the Scots were searching for a way to end their domination by an English king. A group of Scottish nobles sent a letter to Pope John XXII requesting him to rescind papal recognition of England's Edward II as King of Scotland and instead give his blessing to Robert the Bruce as the rightful ruler of Scotland.

Jefferson had read the Declaration of Arbroath in the original Latin and remembered its litany of Edward II's abuses:

"The deeds of cruelty, massacre, violence, pillage, arson, imprisoning prelates, burning down monasteries, robbing and killing monks and nuns and yet other outrages without number which he committed against our people, sparing neither age nor sex, religion nor rank, no-one could describe nor fully imagine unless he had seen them with his own eyes."

Jefferson noted the Arbroath Declaration contained a list of royal abuses. Such a list was useful for his own current project. That declaration however was not really about independence.

The Scottish Barons had requested a single man, the pope, to give his blessing to replace one monarch with another. Jefferson's American audience was much larger and America was not looking for a new monarch. Arbroath was not a model for the status of the American mind.

Considering the papal involvement in both *Magna Carta* and Arbroath reinforced for Jefferson the import of his proposed clause for Virginia's constitution: *"All persons shall have full and free liberty of religious opinion..."* Whatever the pope's role in the world, it should not include decisions of government.

The Dutch Act of Abjuration
Plakkaat van Verlatinghe

During his meeting at City Tavern with Adams the day before, the Dutch experience of 1581 had also crossed his mind.

In 1581, the Netherlands were ruled by King Philip of Spain. The council of the Netherlands provinces passed the *Plakkaat van Verlatinghe,* known in English as the Act of Abjuration.

The act contended that King Philip, by his conduct, had given up or "abjured" his right to be the sovereign power over the Netherlands. It too contained a list of the king's abuses. The disputes involved religious controversy as well.

The Netherlands declared they would be exchanging the rule of one sovereign (King Philip of Spain) for the rule of another (Duke of Anjou who was the brother of the King of France).

While Jefferson recognized that the Dutch had not sought true independence, the idea that a king's conduct could make his rule illegitimate was one that would have value in the American declaration.

That had been a developing theme in America and reflective of the American Mind. He made a note to incorporate that thought into the declaration.

The 1689 English Bill of Rights

The last potential precedent from history for Jefferson to consider was the 1689 English Bill of Rights. John Dickinson was fond of referring to this as part of the English tradition guaranteeing the rights of Englishmen.

Jefferson and Richard Henry Lee had discussed this as well. That agreement between England's aristocracy and a Dutch invader hardly protected Americans if indeed it possessed any real value to Englishmen.

The aristocracy had "invited" the Protestant Willem to invade and depose the Catholic King James. This "Bill of Rights" was another example of the dangers of religion in government, and a supposed declaration that in reality was meant to secure the status of the ruling class.

Jefferson considered the events that had placed the Dutch Willem (who would change his Dutch name to the more English William) and his wife on the English throne. They would reign as King William and Queen Mary. He noted the small irony in his dismissal of the 1689 English Bill of Rights.

The place where Jefferson had studied and honed the analytical skills he was bringing to bear at this moment, William and Mary College, had been named after the Dutch invader and his English bride who had deposed her father.

Was there value in these historical "precedents"?

Jefferson noted patterns in the possible historical precedents. Each instance had a religious element. Each included an effort to replace one despotic royal sovereign with another despotic royal sovereign. While the records of these disputes over power employed terms like "rights" and "liberties", it was clear the goal of each was to enhance or secure the place of an established nobility or upper class.

While these events and documents contained lessons, they were not precedents for the contemplated American action. Beyond the list of grievances, these documents were not remotely related to the American Mind.

It was clear however that the commonality of a list of grievances against the sovereign personally and the arguments that a king had forfeited his right to rule served a clear purpose. These concepts belonged in his draft declaration.

The inclusion of grievance lists and statements of royal forfeiture of the right to rule were the manner in which a revolution was announced. Americans were announcing a revolution.

Thomas Jefferson had begun his preparation to draft the announcement that America was in revolt against England by recalling historical announcements of revolution. It was clear that for the world audience to understand Jefferson would need to list the king's crimes and how by those crimes the king no longer had the right to rule.

Those ideas would be understood by international readers of the declaration and allow them to support the revolution, since it would no longer be a civil war within the British Empire, but a war between two sovereign nations.

David J. Shestokas

Defining the American Mind

There was another, more important audience: the American people. For that audience, the declaration had an entirely different task.

For the American people, the declaration did not have to educate or convince, but rather to express on their behalf what they already felt and believed.

Tracing the Development of the American Mind

Jefferson had come of age as America was developing a mind of its own. Attorney James Otis' 1760 court arguments opposing British searches of colonial property in the Writs of Assistance cases had become well known. Otis had advanced the principle that there was a higher law that governed governments as well as people.

Otis' arguments contained the seeds of what had now become the prevailing thought in America. Otis' pamphlet of 1762, *A Vindication of the Conduct of the House of Representatives* relied abundantly on John Locke's *Second Treatise of Government* and its principles of natural law.

Otis argued natural law was above the law of the "unwritten" British constitution. Otis was a messenger for freedom, though *Vindication* was sprinkled with compliments for the king. While *Vindication* had compliments for King George, Otis' also asserted that the people possessed a "right of revolution".

In asserting a right of revolution Otis brought John Locke's philosophy to the attention of the colonists and over the next sixteen years Americans had made Locke's ideas of a sovereign individual consenting to a limited government their own.

During these past sixteen years Jefferson had not only studied Otis and Locke, he had been a participant in events and made his own contributions to the American Mind.

Jefferson's treatise, *A Summary View of the Rights of British North America,* had been one contribution. His education and experience helped him to recognize the sense of the American people that the declaration would need to express. American thought on British rule had evolved over time, with many contributors to that evolution.

John Dickinson, although he seemed a current political stumbling block to independence, had contributed. Dickinson's series of twelve essays, *Letters from a Farmer in Pennsylvania,* published in

1767-68, questioned British authority and hinted at armed conflict.

The essays had brought Dickinson fame and respect. Using points from those essays would contribute to the success of Jefferson's draft declaration. Dickinson and those who respected him were an important part of the declaration's intended audience.

Jefferson made notes of other influences on the American Mind. The notes showed the development of American thinking. Jefferson started with James Otis and his own experiences in the Virginia legislature. From the fiery oratory of fellow Virginian Patrick Henry, to the many newspaper essays and pamphlets in circulation, the evidence of how Americans thought about government, and their growing restlessness under British rule was everywhere. There were two pieces of evidence that were recent and influential.

Jefferson considered how the hugely popular pamphlet by Thomas Paine, *Common Sense,* both reflected and educated its readers. Paine had written what hundreds of thousands of Americans were thinking, and sold hundreds of thousands of pamphlets. Paine's readers had their thoughts confirmed and gained the tools they needed to arouse or inspire others. Providing further tools would be part of the declaration's purpose.

Then, just yesterday, the *Pennsylvania Gazette's* June 12, 1776 edition published an item that reminded Jefferson why he wished he were in Virginia. George Mason and a committee of the Virginia Convention had created Virginia's Declaration of Rights as part of the process involved in designing the state's constitution. The *Gazette* had published a proposed draft of Virginia's Declaration. It contained elements of the developed American Mind and began:

Virginia Declaration of Rights

I That all men are by nature equally free and independent, and have certain inherent rights, of which, when they enter into a state of society, they cannot, by any compact, deprive or divest their posterity; namely, the enjoyment of life and liberty, with the means of acquiring and possessing property, and pursuing and obtaining happiness and safety.

II That all power is vested in, and consequently derived from, the people; that magistrates are their trustees and servants, and at all times amenable to them.

III That government is, or ought to be, instituted for the common benefit, protection, and security of the people, nation or community; of all the various modes and forms of government that is best, which is capable of producing the greatest degree of happiness and safety and is most effectually secured against the danger of maladministration; and that, whenever any government shall be found inadequate or contrary to these purposes, a majority of the community hath an indubitable, unalienable, and indefeasible right to reform, alter or abolish it, in such manner as shall be judged most conducive to the public weal.

Jefferson recognized that The Virginia Declaration of Rights expressed many principles that had become part of the uniquely American concept of government.

The Virginia Declaration began with a belief in the equality of men and that all men possessed rights that no government could take away, nor could any man give away these rights.

The next American principle Virginia's Declaration announces is that government officials are the servants of the people and serve with the people's consent.

Virginia, in Part III, also recognizes that the people possess a most critical right in the event that government interferes with the exercise of the people's inherent rights or its officials fail to serve the people: *The Right of Revolution.*

David J. Shestokas

The End of a Long Few Days

He had agreed upon an outline with John Adams of the declaration to explain to the world the reasons for American independence. Having completed his notes on the evolution and current state of, as he called it, the American Mind, putting meat on the skeleton of the outline would be Jefferson's next challenge. That would need to wait until tomorrow. He picked up his violin to clear his mind so that he might sleep.

The Second Continental Congress was scheduled to open its Friday, June 14, 1776 session at 10 AM. While Thomas Jefferson was expected to attend he would not. He had spent a restless night with his own mind contemplating the task that had fallen to him.

It was exactly one week since his fellow Virginian, Richard Henry Lee had officially proposed a resolution for American independence to the Congress. For various reasons and quirks of fate, Jefferson's role in this historic drama now loomed large. Jefferson thought back on the events of the last few days.

On June 11th, Ben Franklin had nominated Jefferson as the Virginian to be on a committee to draw up a declaration to explain the choice of independence to England, the nations of the world (particularly potential foreign allies), the Continental Army and the American people. The committee needed a Virginian, as it was Virginia's resolution, and Lee had had to leave Philadelphia to tend to his sick wife.

On June 12th, Franklin's nomination became an appointment and that evening Jefferson headed to City Tavern expecting to take part in a meeting of the Declaration Committee with John Adams, Franklin, Roger Sherman and Roger Livingston. The meeting surprisingly was just Jefferson and Adams.

It was clear at that moment few thought the declaration to be terribly important. Over dinner, he and Adams, agreed to a fairly simple form for the declaration:

    1. A preamble or "whereas" statement explaining the purpose of the document

    2. A statement of law/philosophy that states the basis for the proposed action

    3. A list of grievances against the king

    4. Prior actions taken in response to the king's acts.

    5. Apply the law/philosophy to the actions to arrive at the conclusion that independence is the appropriate remedy to the grievances.

On the 13th, Jefferson was "assigned" by Adams to draft the declaration to justify independence. His first order of business was to consider what was needed to effectively fill in the outline he had arrived at with Adams. This involved lessons from history and sharpening his sense of the thinking of the American people. Tomorrow it would be time to start writing.

David J. Shestokas

Setting Quill to Parchment

The International Audience for the Declaration of Independence

Jefferson reviewed his notes from the day before. It was clear that for the foreign audience he had to weave in the abuses of the king and how those abuses had resulted in the king giving up any legitimate claim to govern the colonies. These points were crucial if there were any hope of assistance from the French or Spanish. This was language they would understand, and then not be taking sides in the internal affairs of the British Empire.

Reading the Mind of the American Audience

The American audience was more complex. It included not only the political leaders, but farmers, shopkeepers, General Washington's army and potential recruits as well.

There was evidence that over the last 16 years a consensus had built among Americans that Jefferson referred to as the "American Mind". The declaration's job for the American audience was not to convince the people of the justness of independence, but rather to confirm for them what they believed.

He had made notes last night on the evolution and current state of the American Mind to guide him in his work.

Looking at his notes on American public statements, essays and writings from James Otis to John Dickinson and his own *Summary View of the Rights of British America* he discerned common themes.

One commonality was a view of natural rights that envisioned rights that belonged to all and extended well beyond the "rights of Englishmen". Another common theme that he discerned in American public acts and statements on government was the existence of a "right of revolution". The last feature of most American writings on British government in the colonies over the last 16 years was the inclusion of a deferential and respectful reference to the king. This element had recently changed in a most dramatic fashion.

James Otis had made respectful references to the king in his *Vindication* as had Dickinson in his *Farmer* letters. Otis included this show of royal respect even while he complained of British Rule, thus outwardly keeping his complaints from sounding like treason.

From 1760 to this day, nearly all public statements about British mistreatment of the colonists included a kind word for "his majesty". This may have been from caution because the punishment for treason could include beheading. Perhaps a few complimented the king because of sincere hopes to reconcile with the mother country.

The American Mind Becomes a Mind of Its Own

There were recent departures from a continued reverence for the king. Patrick Henry made clear he had no hopes of reconciliation in 1774 when he called King George a tyrant and invited the king's assassination. Thomas Paine's *Common Sense* not only had no kind words for George, he declared no king had a right to rule. Paine's pamphlet was wildly popular, with estimates of over 100,000 copies in circulation in the first six months of 1776. The American Mind had been preparing to discard royal deference and publicly express its grievances against the king himself. For Jefferson it appeared the preparation was now complete.

The American Mind had passed the last hurdle to become a mind completely of its own, unlike any in history and exceptional.

How to Begin?

Jefferson's job was now to find the words to convey the common sense of the matter to the world and the American people. He grabbed his goose quill and dipped it in the ink.

The lawyer in Jefferson took over. This was to be a legal document. Legal documents had a form and structure. Such documents typically began with a **"WHEREAS...."** Jefferson anticipated that this declaration would be read aloud at public gatherings. "Whereas" had a conspicuously *royal* tone to it, particularly when read aloud in public. Americans were announcing a revolution against a king. Using a word like "whereas" that had the sound of an order from a monarch would set a poor tone. Jefferson needed to open without using "whereas".

Since the goal was to reflect the American common sense on the justness of independence, the first phrase must set the tone that what was to follow was obvious. After mentally playing with words, and saying them aloud it struck him.

Jefferson considered for a moment that he was going to be joining Richard Henry Lee and John Adams as a candidate for hanging, burning and mutilation and beheading. He placed the inked quill upon the parchment...

Creating the Declaration of Independence

"When in the course of human events..."

David J. Shestokas

Jefferson the Lawyer at Work

While the Declaration of Independence is revered for its eloquence, and inspirational philosophies, in the most straightforward sense it is a legal document written by a lawyer and approved by lawyers. Of the Declaration's signers 25 of 56 were lawyers. Of the non-lawyers, the rest were in business and active in public affairs.

The statistics are often mentioned, but the import of the statistics is almost never discussed. When you keep this commonality in mind, the form of the document makes sense.

The principle author, Thomas Jefferson, was admitted to practice law at age of 24 and drafted the Declaration of Independence at youthful 33 years old.

Good Lawyers Imitate and Improvise

Here's something about lawyers: Good lawyers imitate and improvise. We have a form for everything: real estate contracts, deeds, wills, answers to discovery, etc. All these forms are collected by topic and placed in a binder and we call them form books.

These days of course, it's even simpler with most of the forms on a CD or in the cloud. While language has changed, lawyers in the 18th Century had form books, and strangely enough, many of the standard legal forms have changed very little in over 240 years, since lawyers continue to imitate and improvise.

A close look at the Declaration of Independence, reveals what Jefferson did: That is to imitate, improvise and fit it into a presentation found in one of his form books.

The USA vs. King George. Or as we know it, the Declaration of Independence

Think about this. The Declaration of Independence so resembles a legal complaint, the title very well could have been, The United States vs. King George.

While five men were on the committee to draft the Declaration, Jefferson largely did the drafting alone, and if he did not have a "form book" with him, he certainly had the form in his mind.

The Elements of a Legal Complaint

A "complaint" is filed in court to start the legal process, whether it is a civil lawsuit, or a criminal prosecution. A complaint contains the elements that Adams and Jefferson, both lawyers, had agreed upon at their initial meeting:

1. • A "whereas" statement explaining the purpose of the document
2. • A statement of law that applies to the matter
3. • A statement describing the conduct of the defendant
4. • A statement describing the conduct of the plaintiff.
5. • A conclusion that applies the law to the parties conduct, and the proper remedy for the conduct.
6. Signature of the Plaintiff

Elements of the Declaration of Independence

A close look at the form of The Declaration of Independence reveals all the elements of a complaint:

1. "When in the Course of Human Events" (Jefferson thought "WHEREAS" sounded too much like a regal decree and these men were announcing a revolution.

2. Jefferson's statement of law is in two parts, first the invocation of the law of nature and nature's God, and second the "self-evident" truths that flow from the law of nature and nature's God: the law of natural, inalienable rights, government purpose and the required consent of the governed.

3. The list of grievances against King George is the conduct of the defendant.

4. "The most humble petitions" to the King from the colonists paint the plaintiffs in a good light.

5. Applying the law to the facts, there is only one possible remedy: Independence

6. Signature of the Plaintiffs: Pledging their lives, their fortunes and their sacred honor. (A very big deal at a time when the penalty for treason was beheading and burning).

This analysis is not intended to diminish Jefferson's work. In 2017, as noted in the beginning there are 194 countries in the world and over 100 of those announced their existence with documents modeled on the Declaration of Independence. The eloquence and eternal values expressed in the Declaration have changed the world, but the format preexisted the Declaration and is used daily in courtrooms around the world in the 21st Century.

With luck you have not had a chance to look closely at a document that starts a lawsuit. If you ever do, and you hold the legal complaint side by side with the Declaration of Independence, you will see this is the form Jefferson followed.

He distilled a century of enlightenment thinking into one remarkable sentence of 55 words that began: *"We hold these truths to be self-evident..."*

He gave us our creed. A lot of nations have emerged from the mists of history and their basic identity is tribal, that is rooted in groups bonded by common blood relatives. Ours is rooted in a great assent, the assent to certain propositions. We are a nation dedicated to a proposition, Jefferson wrote the proposition, and as Lincoln said preserved it forever.

Jefferson did more than write an inspirational creed. In using the legal form of a complaint he provided a statement of law.

David J. Shestokas

Eight Other Important Words

From "When in the course of human events" through "our sacred honor", the text of the Declaration of Independence is 1,323 words. Abraham Lincoln praised 55 words in particular that have become a stumbling block to tyranny since they were written. There are eight other words in the Declaration of Independence as critical as those stating the American Creed: ""*the Law of Nature and of Nature's God...*" That phrase would become the legal justification for the existence of the United States.

The Statement of Law

Jefferson the lawyer needed a statement of law for his complaint against King George. The statement of law needed to have power and to provide the authority for the self-evident truth that all men are created equal with inalienable rights, and express a legitimate legal authority for independence. Through human history, government had obtained authority, if not always legitimacy, by relying on a religious claim of right, exercising physical force and violence or a combination of both. The Declaration of Independence proclaimed that the United States was to be different.

The United States was to be a nation of laws. It was not simply going to be a group of men claiming a legal monopoly on the use of violence or relying primarily upon a deity to claim a right to rule. Considering that goal, the Declaration of Independence needed to include a statement of legal authority beyond that of men.

The "self-evident" truths in the Declaration of Independence are derived from *"the Law of Nature and of Nature's God . . ."* Jefferson expressed in those eight words the crucial difference of the United States in relation to all that had gone before.

Years later, the Natural Law which Jefferson cited would find recognition in the Constitution. That recognition was critical in constructing the Constitution to balance the need for an organized society and every individual's natural desire for freedom. Understanding the connection between the Constitution and the Declaration of Independence reveals the Declaration's lasting effect on our daily lives.

The United States was founded on a philosophy of law. That legal philosophy contained the truths that human beings are equal in their possession of natural rights, such as the rights to life, liberty and the fruits of their labor. For the country to be one of law, there had to be a law that was beyond the ability of men to change. *"The Law of Nature and of Nature's God"* is such a law. The Constitution would later become a set of rules to execute the statement of law Jefferson wrote into the Declaration of Independence.

David J. Shestokas

The "Law of Nature and Nature's God"

"Natural Law", at its simplest, recognizes that there exist in the world things that no man, therefore no government, since government derives its power from a grant from men, has any power to change. Though a government might pass a law that says the Law of Gravity will be repealed in its territory, clearly the government's law will be without effect. In the same way, a law that commands a citizen to give up the desire to be free will be ineffective. Gravity and the aspiration for freedom are simply beyond the power of a legislature to change. This idea is the essence of Natural Law.

Jefferson combined the two sources of Natural Law in those eight words. The Law of Nature can be observed in a scientific, secular sense. The Law of Nature's God is revealed to men in a spiritual, divine sense. Whether a particular individual relies upon scientific observation or revelation from God, the final conclusion is the same: all men have inalienable rights. Combining that thought into a single phrase is yet another example of Jefferson's ability to do in few words what others take whole books to explain.

The Basis of Government Authority

For a government to survive and function it needs a basis to exercise authority over people. Government will only function as long as its citizens accept its authority. A government that lacks or loses the acceptance of the people over whom it exercises authority will not endure. Over human history, before the Declaration of Independence, acceptance was garnered through combinations of fear and tradition.

Dictators, whether labeled king, czar, sultan, chief, emperor or general, obtain authority by instilling fear of disobedience in the populace. A theocracy ordained by God arises from religious traditions. A monarchy combines fear of the monarch's absolute authority and religious traditions. The idea of a Divine Right of Kings rests upon the explanation that God works His will to appoint the monarch. To disobey the monarch is to disobey God.

Before the Declaration's reliance upon Natural Law, people's acceptance of a government was dictated by the fear of punishment, whether in this life or the next. In either event, rule was imposed upon the people by threat.

Jefferson's propositions of law rejected that and recognized that the proper natural order gave no one the right to govern others without their consent. Many years later he would say that he was simply explaining the common sense of the matter. The only people for whom the idea would not be common sense were and are those who thought they were in fact better than others with a natural right to rule. The philosophy of Natural Law expressed in the Declaration of Independence as the only source of legitimate legal authority for government has been a thorn for would be despots and tyrants ever since.

Government by Philosophy: Understanding, Acceptance & Consistent Conduct

The United States was founded as a government that would not have a dictator or king. The United States would not exercise authority over the population through threat, but rather through consent. There are prerequisites to obtaining and maintaining consent.

For a government without a dictator or king, benevolent or otherwise, to survive it must have a central philosophy. For a government founded on philosophy to maintain its authority, four things are needed:

1. An understanding by the people of the philosophy
2. An acceptance by the people of the philosophy
3. Conduct by the government consistent with the philosophy
4. Consent of the Governed

The Declaration of Independence Established Natural Law as the Organizing Principle of the United States

As announced in the Declaration of Independence, the founding philosophical, legal and organizing principle of the United States is Natural Law. The announcement was in Jefferson's statement of law in the complaint against King George. That statement of law contained two propositions. The first proposition of law is found in the very beginning:

"When in the Course of human events it becomes necessary for one people ... to assume among the powers of the earth, the separate and equal station to which the **Laws of Nature and of Nature's God** *entitle them ..."*

The second proposition are the 55 words discussed in the introduction, but bear repeating as the emphasis before was not on their legal effect, but their status as a statement of the

American Creed. Consider now the 55 words as Jefferson's succinct summary of the central principles of Natural Law in a manner designed to be understood by the American people:

"We hold these truths to be self-evident: that all men are created equal, that they are endowed by their Creator with certain unalienable Rights, that among these are Life, Liberty and the pursuit of Happiness.--That to secure these rights, Governments are instituted among Men, deriving their just powers from the consent of the governed."

That the people understood and accepted the philosophy is best demonstrated by the fact that by the end of the Revolution in 1783, there would be 8,000 Americans killed in battle and 217,000 would serve in the Continental Army. Considering the population was about 2,500,000 in 1776, the equivalent in 2017 would be 1,056,000 killed and 28,644,000 in the service.

By invoking the "Laws of Nature and of Nature's God" Jefferson and the Declaration's 55 other signers committed the new country to a legal standard of freedom to be incorporated into the forms of government that would follow. Ultimately the Constitution would complete the process by obtaining formal "consent of the governed" through the ratification process during the period of 1787-1791. The Bill of Rights, ratified in 1791 completed the original Founding process.

Submitting the Constitution for ratification by the people and formally recognizing inalienable rights in the nation's organic law were government conduct consistent with the philosophy defined in the Declaration of Independence.

Jefferson's statement of Natural Law launched the country in that direction and committed its leaders to obtaining the people's consent. What was the source of Jefferson's statement of law?

Understanding the Definitions of Natural Law: Divine and Secular

The two components of the Law of Nature and Nature's God are secular and divine. Divine Natural Law has been revealed or inspired by God, or another supreme, supernatural being. Secular Natural Law is the consequence of nature's physical, biological, and behavioral laws that can be observed and measured by the human mind. Divine and Secular Natural Law have fixed principles that are beyond the manipulation of men.

Divine Natural Law

Divine Natural Law is discerned from revelations and inspiration by a power greater than humanity. In Judeo-Christian tradition, The Bible and Torah reveal Divine Natural Law in the writings of divinely inspired authors. The legitimacy of enacted human law is measured by the degree to which the law is in agreement and harmony with divinely revealed principles of right and wrong. Human laws inconsistent with divine principles of morality are invalid and should neither be enforced nor obeyed. St. Thomas Aquinas, a theologian and philosopher from the thirteenth century, laid the ground work for defining Divine Natural Law.

Aquinas advanced the idea of *imago Dei*, that human beings were created in God's image. The result of Aquinas' thought was that human beings are all equal in worth in relation to each other and that in any pyramid of value human beings are uniquely valuable. These are divine revelations of universal truths. Human rights as revealed by Divine Natural Law are considered to be:

1. Inherent
2. Inalienable
3. Indivisible
4. Universal

In this view, Divine Natural Rights are the birth right of each human being and can neither be taken away nor given away.

Secular Natural Law

Secular Natural Law recognizes there are immutable laws of nature. There are things in the physical world that are unchangeable. Examples are biology, motion, gravity, optics, and mechanics as noted by Sir William Blackstone, an eighteenth century English lawyer whose writings were widely read by the Founders, including Jefferson.

Blackstone recognized that there are physical laws which are observable and measureable. Observing and measuring the physical world through the prism of human intellect reveals reliable truths about the world. Such reliable truths exist regarding human nature.

Secular Natural Law relies upon observations and measurements of human nature that exist regardless of any activity by government. Secular Natural Law identifies uniform and fixed moral and ethical norms. A government attempt to interfere with these fixed elements of the human condition will have no more effect than a decree that gravity will not apply in its territory. Inalienable and immutable human rights flow from human nature and exist independent of government.

John Locke, an English philosopher whose 1689 *Second Treatise of Government* influenced Jefferson's ideas and writing, observed the fixed elements of human nature include: liberty, equality and self-preservation. In the natural order of things, absent government, every individual possesses a right of self-preservation exercised on an equal basis with all others. Self-preservation inherently includes fulfillment of personal needs consistent with the liberties of others.

Human nature also includes elements like greed and narcissism inconsistent with the liberties of others. To address this inconsistency, people establish government to protect life, liberty, and property. Government comports with Secular Natural Law when it provides those protections. Government authority derives from consent to provide those protections. Government actions beyond that consent are illegitimate.

Combining Divine and Secular Natural Law

Jefferson recognized that the law of nature and Nature's God arrived at the same result and eloquently combined them to state the legal basis for the legitimacy of the United States in the Declaration of Independence.

Creating the Declaration of Independence

Recognition of Unenumerated Natural Rights in the U.S. Constitution

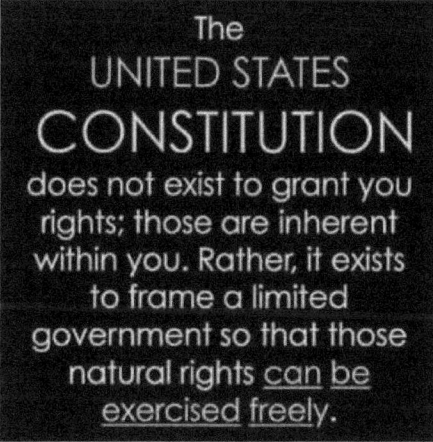

The Declaration of Independence affirmatively states the legal basis of the United States is Natural Law. The Declaration intertwines Secular Natural Law ("Laws of Nature") and Divine Natural Law ("Nature's God"). The two are compatible. Although each begins with a different premise, they each wind up in the same place. "Thou shall not kill" being a Divine commandment revealed to Moses, and the Right to Life being an immutable law of nature as observed by Locke is a simple example.

Law written by men is referred to as "positive law", distinguishing it from Natural Law. The United States Constitution is an example of positive law. Through the Constitution specific inalienable natural rights have been made part of the country's positive law in the Bill of Rights. These include: freedom of speech, religion and press, and the right to keep and bear arms.

Though there are specific natural rights recognized and written into the positive law that is the Constitution the Founders understood that it was impossible to list each and every right inherently belonging to every human being. As a result of the country's Natural Law heritage the Constitution specifically recognizes the existence of rights not listed in the document. This can be traced to Jefferson's statement of law in the Declaration of Independence.

Rights that Go Beyond the Constitution

The Declaration's affirmation of Natural Law as the legal basis for the country leads to recognition of rights beyond those stated in the Constitution, or unenumerated rights. This recognition took the form of positive law most firmly stated in the Ninth Amendment:

"The enumeration in the Constitution, of certain rights, shall not be construed to deny or disparage others retained by the people."

This provision recognizes that rights exist outside the written positive law. This principle, arising from Natural Law, expressed in the Declaration of Independence, provides the organizing philosophy for the United States government, its legal legitimacy and constraints upon its actions.

Natural Law Heritage in Action at the Supreme Court

When the Supreme Court looks to Founding and organizing principles of Natural Rights/Natural Law, it comes down on the side of liberty. An all too rare example was arriving at the Second Amendment's right to bear arms as a personal and not collective right.

The Supreme Court resolved the "collective" versus "individual" debate in *District of Columbia v. Heller (2008)*. How it did so was unusual. The Court's resolution traced the individual right to bear arms to a natural right that existed prior to the Constitution. For the Court to do such a thing is atypical, but demonstrates the role Natural Law has in limiting and legitimizing the power of government.

In its resolution of a major Second Amendment issue the Court acknowledged that the Founding generation understood there are rights not given by government, but exist independent of it. The right to self-defense is among the inalienable rights alluded to in the Declaration of Independence.

David J. Shestokas

Divine, Secular and Historical Natural Law as Organizing Principles

Both Divine and Secular Natural Law have unyielding principles that can be looked upon for government legitimacy in citizen acceptance of government authority. They provide the basis for a "government of law, not men".

The statement of law that Jefferson incorporated into his legal complaint against King George has had, and continues to have, legal and inspirational impact on American law and the law of countries around the world.

In the End, Simply Common Sense

In 1825, nearly 50 years after he wrote the Declaration of Independence Jefferson, would sum up his goal with writing the Declaration of Independence was "not to find out new principles, or new arguments, never before thought of, not merely to say things which had never been said before; but to place before mankind the common sense of the subject."

The document has inspired millions and analyzed by hundreds of thousands. Jefferson, as he had so often in his life took something apparently complex and expressed it elegantly and simply as "common sense".

AFTERWORD

2017 is the 30th Anniversary of my admission to practice law. The final part of becoming a lawyer is to swear an oath to uphold the Constitution of the United States. As I raised my right hand and placed my left on the-Bible, the thought ran through my mind that at no time during law school was the meaning of this oath explained. I've spent the ensuing thirty years working to figure that out.

What I've discovered is that it is not simply the technical aspects of the Constitution that one is swearing to support. There is an underlying philosophy linked to the Constitution that one must support to truly uphold the Constitution. That philosophy is found in the Declaration of Independence and its self-evident truths that all men are created equal with inalienable rights that we are born with and are not granted by government.

I've discovered that one cannot support the Constitution without study and understanding of the Declaration of Independence.

My first book, **Constitutional Sound Bites**, provides an example of this. That book, while devoted to explaining the Constitution, contains 140 references to the Declaration of Independence.

Since 1987 I've taken the constitutional oath five more times, and each time felt more comfortable as I have studied and gained a deeper understanding of the Declaration. One purpose of *Creating the Declaration of Independence* is to pass along some of that to the millions of others who take such an oath whether attorneys, law enforcement officers, firefighters, elected officials or new citizens.

It seemed one way to do that is to explain the process of creating the Declaration of Independence taking place in the minds of those involved. This book attempts to do that. When the 56 men who signed the Declaration of Independence pledged their lives, fortunes and sacred honor in support of the Declaration it was truly a remarkable act. The possible penalty for that act included being disemboweled, cut into pieces and beheaded.

Can you imagine being the first one to go out on that limb, or the person assigned to convince millions to join? I have tried to conceive of what that must have been like and have had that impression in my mind the times I have been called upon to swear to uphold our Constitution.

APPENDIX

The Declaration of Independence

IN CONGRESS, July 4, 1776.
The unanimous Declaration of the thirteen united States of America,

When in the Course of human events, it becomes necessary for one people to dissolve the political bands which have connected them with another, and to assume among the powers of the earth, the separate and equal station to which the Laws of Nature and of Nature's God entitle them, a decent respect to the opinions of mankind requires that they should declare the causes which impel them to the separation.

We hold these truths to be self-evident, that all men are created equal, that they are endowed by their Creator with certain unalienable Rights, that among these are Life, Liberty and the pursuit of Happiness.--That to secure these rights, Governments are instituted among Men, deriving their just powers from the consent of the governed, --That whenever any Form of Government becomes destructive of these ends, it is the Right of the People to alter or to abolish it, and to institute new Government, laying its foundation on such principles and organizing its powers in such form, as to them shall seem most likely to effect their Safety and Happiness. Prudence, indeed, will dictate that Governments long established should not be changed for light and transient causes; and accordingly all experience hath shewn, that mankind are more disposed to suffer, while evils are sufferable, than to right themselves by abolishing the forms to which they are accustomed. But when a long train of abuses and usurpations, pursuing invariably the same Object evinces a design to reduce them under absolute Despotism, it is their right, it is their duty, to throw off such Government, and to provide new Guards for their future security.--Such has been the patient sufferance of these Colonies; and such is now the necessity which constrains them to alter their former Systems of Government. The history of the present King of Great Britain is a history of repeated injuries and usurpations, all having in direct object the establishment of an absolute Tyranny over these States. To prove this, let Facts be submitted to a candid world.

He has refused his Assent to Laws, the most wholesome and necessary for the public good.

He has forbidden his Governors to pass Laws of immediate and pressing importance, unless suspended in their operation till his Assent should be obtained; and when so suspended, he has utterly neglected to attend to them.

He has refused to pass other Laws for the accommodation of large districts of people, unless those people would relinquish the right of Representation in the Legislature, a right inestimable to them and formidable to tyrants only.

He has called together legislative bodies at places unusual, uncomfortable, and distant from the depository of their public Records, for the sole purpose of fatiguing them into compliance with his measures.

He has dissolved Representative Houses repeatedly, for opposing with manly firmness his invasions on the rights of the people.

He has refused for a long time, after such dissolutions, to cause others to be elected; whereby the Legislative powers, incapable of Annihilation, have returned to the People at large for their exercise; the State remaining in the mean time exposed to all the dangers of invasion from without, and convulsions within.

He has endeavoured to prevent the population of these States; for that purpose obstructing the Laws for Naturalization of Foreigners; refusing to pass others to encourage their migrations hither, and raising the conditions of new Appropriations of Lands.

He has obstructed the Administration of Justice, by refusing his Assent to Laws for establishing Judiciary powers.

He has made Judges dependent on his Will alone, for the tenure of their offices, and the amount and payment of their salaries.

He has erected a multitude of New Offices, and sent hither swarms of Officers to harrass our people, and eat out their substance.

He has kept among us, in times of peace, Standing Armies without the Consent of our legislatures.

He has affected to render the Military independent of and superior to the Civil power.

He has combined with others to subject us to a jurisdiction foreign to our constitution, and unacknowledged by our laws; giving his Assent to their Acts of pretended Legislation:

For Quartering large bodies of armed troops among us:

For protecting them, by a mock Trial, from punishment for any Murders which they should commit on the Inhabitants of these States:

For cutting off our Trade with all parts of the world:

For imposing Taxes on us without our Consent:

For depriving us in many cases, of the benefits of Trial by Jury:

For transporting us beyond Seas to be tried for pretended offences

For abolishing the free System of English Laws in a neighbouring Province, establishing therein an Arbitrary government, and enlarging its Boundaries so as to render it at once an example and fit instrument for introducing the same absolute rule into these Colonies:

For taking away our Charters, abolishing our most valuable Laws, and altering fundamentally the Forms of our Governments:

For suspending our own Legislatures, and declaring themselves invested with power to legislate for us in all cases whatsoever.

He has abdicated Government here, by declaring us out of his Protection and waging War against us.

He has plundered our seas, ravaged our Coasts, burnt our towns, and destroyed the lives of our people.

He is at this time transporting large Armies of foreign Mercenaries to compleat the works of death, desolation and tyranny, already begun with circumstances of Cruelty & perfidy scarcely paralleled in the most barbarous ages, and totally unworthy the Head of a civilized nation.

He has constrained our fellow Citizens taken Captive on the high Seas to bear Arms against their Country, to become the executioners of their friends and Brethren, or to fall themselves by their Hands.

He has excited domestic insurrections amongst us, and has endeavoured to bring on the inhabitants of our frontiers, the merciless Indian Savages, whose known rule of warfare, is an undistinguished destruction of all ages, sexes and conditions.

In every stage of these Oppressions We have Petitioned for Redress in the most humble terms: Our repeated Petitions have been answered only by repeated injury. A Prince whose character is thus marked by every act which may define a Tyrant, is unfit to be the ruler of a free people.

Nor have We been wanting in attentions to our British brethren. We have warned them from time to time of attempts by their legislature to extend an unwarrantable jurisdiction over us. We have reminded them of the circumstances of our emigration and settlement here. We have appealed to their native justice and magnanimity, and we have conjured them by the ties of our common kindred to disavow these usurpations, which, would inevitably interrupt our connections and correspondence. They too have been deaf to the voice of justice and of consanguinity. We must, therefore, acquiesce in the necessity, which denounces our Separation, and hold them, as we hold the rest of mankind, Enemies in War, in Peace Friends.

We, therefore, the Representatives of the united States of America, in General Congress, Assembled, appealing to the Supreme Judge of the world for the rectitude of our intentions, do, in the Name, and by Authority of the good People of these Colonies, solemnly publish and declare, That these United Colonies are, and of Right ought to be Free and Independent States; that they are Absolved from all Allegiance to the British Crown, and that all political connection between them and the State of Great Britain, is and ought to be totally dissolved; and that as Free and Independent States, they have full Power to levy War, conclude Peace, contract Alliances, establish Commerce, and to do all other Acts and Things which Independent States may of right do. And for the support of this Declaration, with a firm reliance on the protection of divine Providence, we mutually pledge to each other our Lives, our Fortunes and our sacred Honor.

John Hancock

David J. Shestokas

Selected Bibliography

I am a voracious reader of the history of the founding of the United States. These are a few of my very favorite books about the Declaration of Independence, the time surrounding its creation and its impact on our country and the world.

Armitage, David, *The Declaration of Independence: A Global History,* Harvard University Press, (2008)

Beck, Derek, *Igniting the American Revolution*, Sourcebooks (2016)

Beck, Derek, *The War Before Independence: 1775-1776,* Sourcebooks (2017)

Ellis, Joseph, *American Creation,* Vintage (2007)

Ellis, Joseph, *Revolutionary Summer: The Birth of American Independence,* Vintage (2013)

Fraden, Dennis, *The Signers: The Fifty-Six Stories Behind the Declaration of Independence*, Walker (2002)

Isaacson, Walter, *Benjamin Franklin: An American Life,* Simon & Schuster (2004)

Maier, Pauline, *American Scripture, Making the Declaration of Independence*, Vintage Books, New York (1997)

McCullough, David, *John Adams,* Simon & Schuster (2002)

McCullough, David, *1776,* Simon & Schuster, (2005)

Sandefur, Timothy, *The Conscience of the Constitution: The Declaration of Independence and the Right to Liberty,* Cato Institute (2015)

St. John, Jeffrey, *Forge of Union, Anvil of Liberty,* Jameson Books Inc.; First edition (June 1992)

Wood, Gordon S., *Revolutionary Characters: What Made the Founders Different,* Penguin Books, Reprint Edition (May 18, 2006)

Creating the Declaration of Independence

David J. Shestokas

About David J. Shestokas

David Shestokas earned his Bachelor of Arts in Political Science from Bradley University and his Juris Doctor from The John Marshall Law School, cum laude, while serving on *The John Marshall Law Review*.

Additionally, he studied comparative legal systems at Trinity College in Dublin, Ireland. He has been admitted to practice law in both state and federal courts in Illinois and Florida.

As a prosecutor and criminal defense attorney for more nearly thirty years, he has lived with the Constitution in the courtroom daily. As an Assistant State's Attorney for Cook County, IL he appeared in court on more than 10,000 criminal prosecutions. While on the Felony Review Unit, he participated in police investigations and made charging decisions in more than 400 felony cases.

In 1992, after the Republic of Lithuania regained its independence from the Soviet Union, Mr. Shestokas joined attorneys of Lithuanian heritage from around the world as a member of the First World Congress of Lithuanian Lawyers.

The Lithuanian President, government officials, and the Lithuanian Bar worked with that Congress to restore the rule of law and a constitutional government after four generations of Soviet occupation.

Mr. Shestokas is the author of the book, **Constitutional Sound Bites,** which grew from his weekly radio show, *Constitutionally Speaking*, and his website, Constitutional Legal Education and News. The website has more than 380,000 annual visitors. His readership is balanced across partisan, economic, ethnic and philosophical persuasions. He resonates with today's readers, be they scholars, teachers, young students, immigrants, history buffs, or the general public, as his style is direct and easy to understand in twenty-first century phrasing; while retaining the integrity of the American Founders.

Along with volunteering at the Salvation Army providing *pro bono* legal services for the homeless, David has also given his time at the Quality Life Center to educate at-risk youth about the values ingrained in America's Founding.

Mr. Shestokas' has also collaborated with Dr. Berta Arias, past President, Illinois Latino Council on Higher Education to produce **Cápsulas Informativas Constitucionales,** the first and only book about the Declaration of Independence, Constitution and Bill of Rights, designed for the 36,000,000 Americans who are more comfortable reading in Spanish.

Join Shestokas' over 100,000 followers on Twitter by following @shestokas. Join the constitutional conversation by being a member of the Dave Shestokas on the Constitution group on Facebook.

Check www.shestokas.com for Shestokas' latest entry in Constitutional Education or commentary on how the Constitution relates to current events.

www.ingramcontent.com/pod-product-compliance
Lightning Source LLC
Chambersburg PA
CBHW021004090426
42738CB00007B/645